CATS KNOW BEST

For Maria's cat, and Tawny Pippet, Ottoline, Nero, and Umblebee.   C.E.

*For Colin, who was inspired to write this book on receiving one of my feline birthday greeting cards.
I also dedicate this book to all my family, especially Evan, James, and Julian, and to my mother,
and to all my cats, past, present, and future.   L.A.I.*

Published by Dial Books
A Division of Penguin Books USA Inc.
375 Hudson Street / New York, New York 10014

Text copyright © 1988 by Colin Eisler / Pictures copyright © 1988 by Lesley Anne Ivory
All rights reserved
Library of Congress Catalog Card Number: 87-15653
Printed in the U.S.A.
First Pied Piper Printing 1992
ISBN 0-14-054857-2
7 9 10 8 6
A Pied Piper Book is a registered trademark of Dial Books for Young Readers,
a division of Penguin Books USA Inc., ® TM 1,163,686 and ® TM 1,054,312.

CATS KNOW BEST
is also published in a hardcover edition by Dial Books.

Some of the cats in this book live with the illustrator, Lesley Anne Ivory.
Their names, from left to right in the order of their appearance, are:

On the front cover: OCTOPUSSY (AGNEATHA's son)
On the title page: AGNEATHA
In front of the fireplace: TAM (MUPPET's son), and BRACKEN and D2 (AGNEATHA's sons)
Keeping cool: GEMMA (mother of MUPPET)
In the drawer: AGNEATHA and her kittens, and TWIGLET under the bed
Drinking milk: TWIGLET, and GABBY in the farmyard
Watching a mouse: TWIGLET again
Nursing her kittens: MUPPET and her kittens (GEMMA's daughter and grandchildren)
Keeping clean: GEMMA on the chair, and AVRIL and APRIL (AGNEATHA's daughters),
and MINOUCHE in the basket with PEEPO
Tidying up: SPIRO (the ginger cat) being groomed by BLOSSOM
Having a good fight: OCTOPUSSY and D2, with HOBOE, a neighbor, on the wall
Moving through the snow: MUPPET and her kittens; GEMMA, the grandmother, is on the windowsill
Playing cat's cradle: RUSKIN
Pretending not to care: CHESTERTON (TWIGLET and GABBY's son)
Looking back: CHESTERTON again
On the back cover: RUSKIN again

CATS KNOW BEST

by COLIN EISLER

pictures by LESLEY ANNE IVORY

A PUFFIN PIED PIPER

Cats know the best places to be.
Where to stay warm…

Or keep cool.

And where to have their kittens.

Cats know the best food.
Where the milk is freshest...

Or the mice most plump.

And how to nurse their kittens.

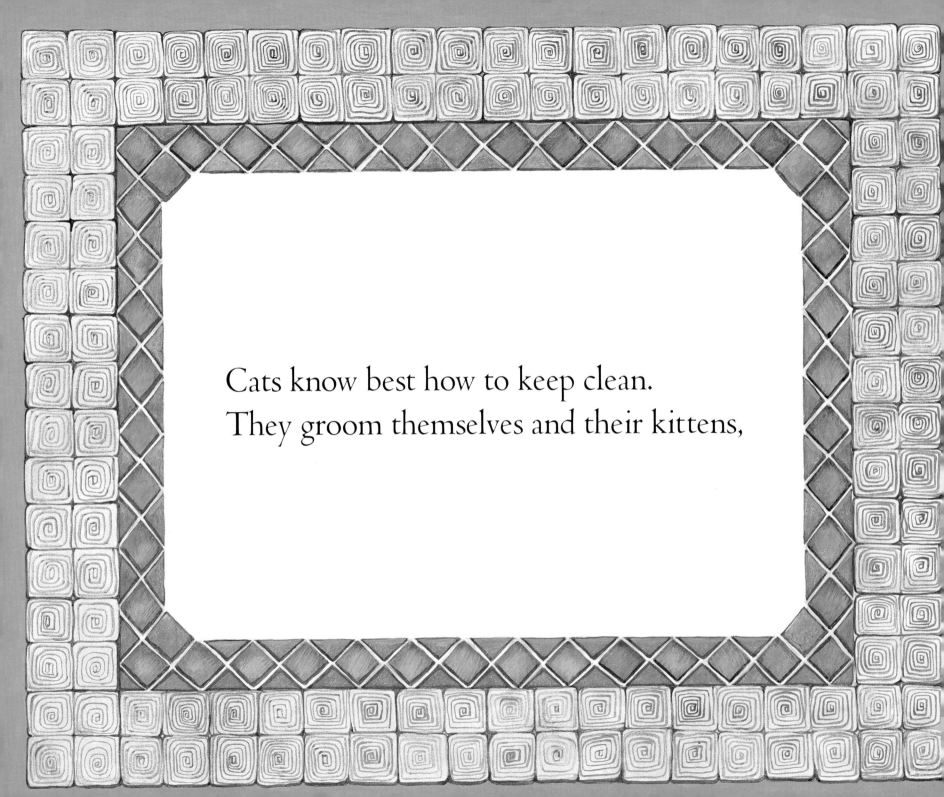

Cats know best how to keep clean.
They groom themselves and their kittens,

Helping each other keep tidy too.

Cats know the best feelings.
They love to have a good fight,
teasing and scrapping,

And caring for their kittens.

Cats know the best games.
They love to play cat's cradle,

And to pretend not to know, or to care,

But they do.

COLIN EISLER,

the distinguished art historian, is Robert Lehman Professor of Fine Arts at the Institute of Fine Arts at New York University. He is the author of many books on art history. His most recent books include: *The Genius of Jacopo Bellini*, *Paintings in the Hermitage*, and *Durer's Animals*. He is also the author of *David's Songs* (Dial), a selection and adaptation of the Psalms, illustrated by Jerry Pinkney. Mr. Eisler is active in the Jewish Museum of New York and the Jewish Heritage Society, and is a Lenten lecturer at the Madison Avenue Presbyterian Church in New York City.

LESLEY ANNE IVORY

has her favorite subjects always nearby to pose for her: The twelve cats that she uses as models make their home with the artist and her husband and their two sons. Well-known for her paintings on cards, calendars, and gifts, Ms. Ivory also illustrated *Meet My Cats* (Dial), said by *School Library Journal* to be "beautifully written...the illustrations finely crafted with rich detail, attractive composition, lush color." Her most recent book for Dial is *Cats in the Sun*.